Baby wakes up

Story by Jenny Giles

Illustrations by Susy Boyer Rigby

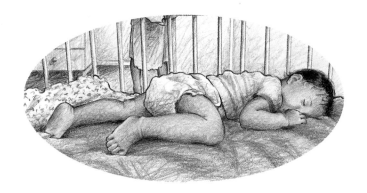

I am up.

Baby is asleep.

3

Mom is asleep.

Dad is asleep.

Baby wakes up.

I look at Baby.

Baby looks at me.

"Look, Baby.

Here is a little teddy bear."

"Look, Baby.

Here is a big teddy bear."

13

Here comes Mom.

"Look, Mom.

Look at Baby."

15

"Baby is happy."